BULLYING

KELLI HICKS

Mitchell Lane
PUBLISHERS

Parent and Caregiver Tips for Creating Nonfiction Readers

Timely topics in the *Dealing With...* series will interest intermediate and middle school readers and equip them with helpful strategies for coping with difficult situations. Your reader will be introduced to new concepts, facts, ideas, and vocabulary.

Tips for Reading Nonfiction

Talk about Nonfiction
Explain that nonfiction books provide facts about real-world topics. When readers read nonfiction, they gain a rich understanding of the world. They build background knowledge that provides a foundation for learning and academic success.

Look at the Parts
This book contains the following helpful features. Share the purpose of each feature with your reader.

Photos, Captions, and Graphic Aids
The photos, captions, charts, and other graphic aids in nonfiction texts contain a wealth of information. Help your reader identify different ways information can be displayed.

Sidebars
These extra tidbits of information help satisfy readers' curiosity and expand their knowledge.

Table of Contents
Located at the front of the book, this list shows the big ideas within the text and the page numbers where they can be found.

Extension Activities and Additional Resources
A "Your Turn" quiz and "Exploration and Discovery" activities invite readers to apply their new knowledge. Supporting resources are provided in a special "You Are Not Alone" section.

Glossary
Located at the back of the book, the glossary defines key words and phrases that are related to the topic. These words and phrases can be found in the text in **bold** type.

Index
Located at the back of the book, the index is an alphabetical list of topics and the page numbers where they can be found.

With a little help and guidance, your reader will be on their way to enjoying and learning from nonfiction books.

Mitchell Lane
PUBLISHERS
mitchelllane.com

2001 SW 31st Avenue
Hallandale, FL 33009

First Edition, 2025.
Author: Kelli Hicks
Designer: Rhea Magaro
Editor: Kim Thompson

Series: Dealing With...
Title: Dealing with Bullying / by Kelli Hicks

Hallandale, FL : Mitchell Lane Publishers, [2025]

Library bound ISBN: 979-8-89260-052-1
eBook ISBN: 979-8-89260-089-7

PHOTO CREDITS
iStock: zoranm, 5; Shutterstock: Pressmaster, cover, 1; Robert Kneschke, 4, 6; Africa Studio, 7, 9, 41, 47; Daniela Barreto, 8; Lopolo, 10, 11; LightField Studios, 12, 40; Dragana Gordic, 13; Dzm1try, 13; pakww, 14; SciePro, 15; Twin Design, 16; Juliya Shangarey, 17; milo827, 18; WeAre, 18; wavebreakmedia, 20, 26; aceshot1, 21; SpeedKingz, 22, 23; Jacob Lund, 24; fizkes, 25; modisketch, 27; veevante, 28; Inside Creative House, 29; PeopleImages.com - Yuri A, 29; Brocreative, 30, 31; Arlene Gapusan, 33; Kamilon, 33; Gatot Adri, 34; Dawn Shearer, 37; M-vector, 38; George Rudy, 39; iofoto, 42; Denis Radovanovic, 44.

Table of Contents

Chapter 1: Mid-Day Misery

Kayla

Kayla skips to the lunchroom. She can't wait to dig into her food and chat with her friends. She is bursting to tell them about the new boy who sat next to her in science class.

Kayla approaches the table where her friends sit every day. "Hey, guys, have you seen the new kid yet?" she asks. Then she realizes something is wrong. The girls aren't looking at her, they didn't save her a seat, and they aren't responding.

"Maria, have you seen the new kid?" Kayla looks from one face to the next. Why are they ignoring her? "Jasmine, did you hear me?" Nothing. "Avery, why didn't you save me a seat?"

Kayla's throat feels tight, and her heart races. "Guys? What's wrong?" Kayla notices the smirks on their faces and the eye roll by Maria. She feels tears well up. She doesn't want to cry in the middle of the cafeteria. As Kayla turns away, she hears laughter. Her heart feels broken. Kayla runs toward the hall to find a quiet place to eat alone.

Jason

In the hallway, Kayla sees her classmate Jason standing face-to-face with an older boy. Suddenly, the taller boy shoves Jason into the wall. *Bam!* "Stay out of my way, shrimp!" he says. "Don't make me have to hurt you!" Jason is shaking. He looks scared.

Sometimes it feels like heartbreak. Sometimes it feels like a physical attack. Either way you look at it, it's bullying.

What Do You Think?

- How did Kayla feel when her friends ignored her? Have you ever been in a similar situation?
- How do you think Jason felt in the hallway?
- What would you have done if you had walked by and seen Jason in trouble?

Chapter 2: What Is Bullying?

Bullying is uninvited, **aggressive** action toward a particular person or group. Bullying tends to repeat over time.

A bully is forceful, and their words and behaviors are meant to cause harm. A bully wants to be in control and works hard to make the **victim** feel powerless. Bullies often pick on the same people over and over.

Types of Bullying

Social Bullying

Social bullying happens when the bully hurts someone by damaging their relationships or attacking their reputation. Think about what happened to Kayla. She thought those girls were her friends, but they ignored her and laughed at her. They made her feel sad and **self-conscious**. The girls wanted to embarrass her. They left her out on purpose. Kayla was the **target** of social bullying. This type of bullying is often experienced by girls.

Verbal Bullying

Verbal bullying happens when the bully hurts someone with words. The bully may threaten or tease the victim. They might call names or use insults. The bully's words are meant to **intimidate**. It can be scary and upsetting to constantly hear taunts and put-downs. Like social bullying, this type of bullying is often experienced by girls.

Physical Bullying

Physical bullying happens when the bully hurts someone by touching them or their belongings. The bully might hit, kick, push, or trip. They might steal or break someone's things. They might threaten physical harm. Think about what happened to Jason in the hallway. After the **violent** attack, he felt pain and fear. This type of bullying is often **instigated** among boys.

Did You Know?

Victims often experience several types of bullying in combination. Bullies want to hurt others, and they will use whatever methods are available.

Cyberbullying

Cyberbullying happens when the bully hurts someone by using the internet and social media platforms to cause embarrassment and harm by posting hurtful photos, videos, or comments. Many kids have 24-hour-a-day access to online gaming and social media accounts. Because of this, cyberbullying can happen anywhere, at any time of the day or night.

- 49 percent of students in grades 4 through 12 have been bullied at least once.
- 71 percent of students have seen others being bullied at school.
- About 30 percent of young people have bullied others at least once.

Bullying and the Brain

Scientists and researchers report that long-term bullying can have a negative impact on your brain. That's because bullying causes **stress**.

Stress is uncomfortable and hard to ignore. It may feel like constant worrying and fear. It can upset your stomach and make your heart beat faster. It can make you feel dizzy. Over time, stress can cause harmful inflammation in your body. It can even change your **hormone** levels. In particular, it can increase the amount of the hormone **cortisol** in your brain.

The **hippocampus** is the part of your brain that is in charge of emotions, learning, and memory. And it does not respond well to high levels of cortisol. Dealing with constant stress can shrink the size of the hippocampus. It can cause memory problems. As a result, victims of long-term bullying may face challenges with learning, concentrating, and remembering the details of an event.

There IS Good News!

Studies show that your brain has the ability to recover from damage caused by bullying and stress. The sooner a person gets help, the sooner the brain can begin the process of healing.

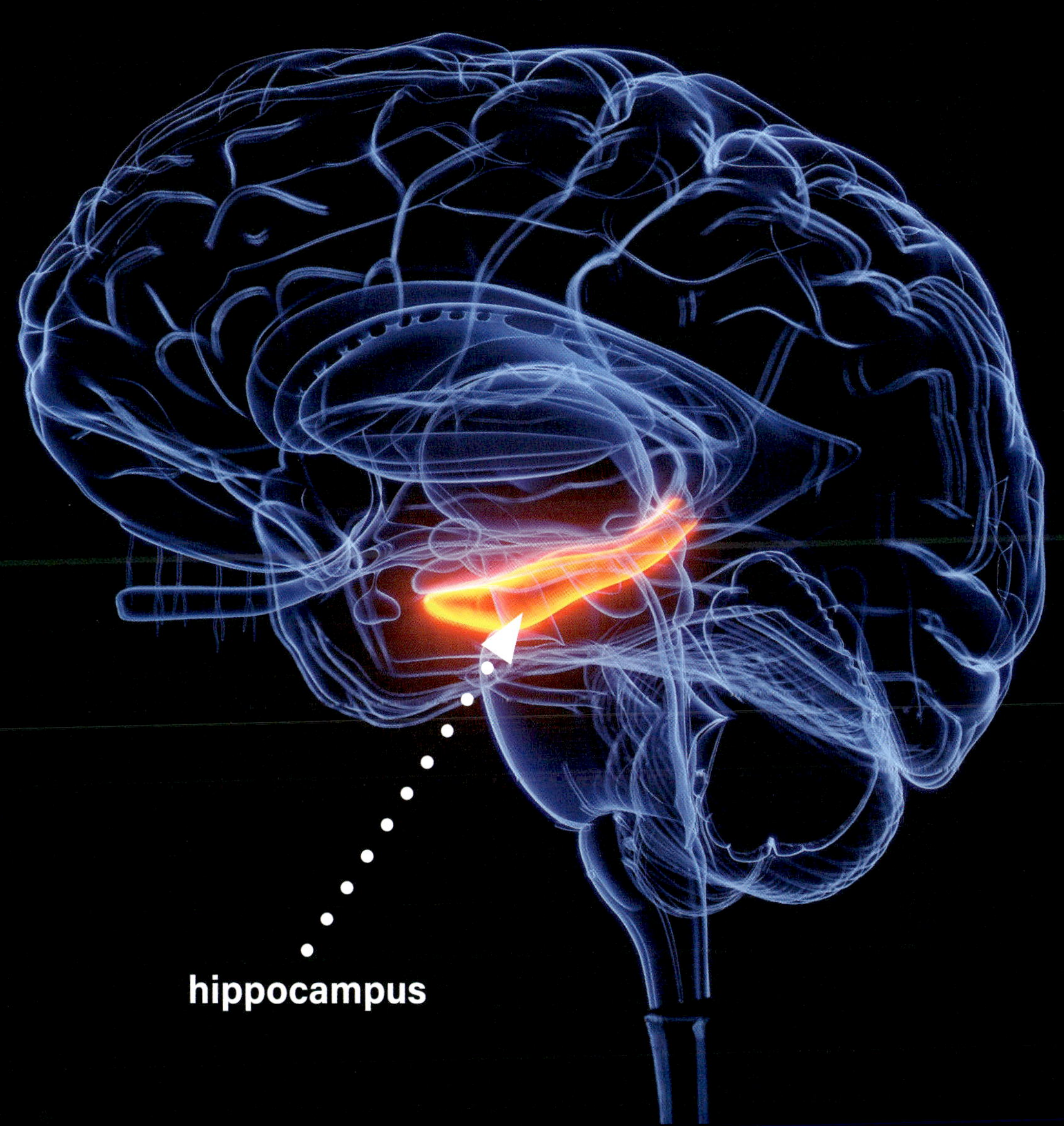

Bullying and Individual Differences

How does a bully decide who their target is going to be? Bullies want to feel powerful. So they usually pick on kids who are believed to have a weakness or who might not be able to defend themselves.

Often, a bully will target a person who is different in some way. The victim might look different than the average student or have beliefs that might be misunderstood. They might learn differently in the classroom or act differently in the hallways.

Many bullies have been bullied themselves in the past. In order to gain control, they become **aggressors**. They think that if they bully others, then no one will pick on them. Sometimes, kids become bullies to impress their friends.

Chapter 3: Signs of Bullying

How can you tell if someone is being bullied? There are many signs to look for. Often, people who are being bullied don't want to go to school, even if they loved it before. They might pretend to be sick. They might get real headaches or stomachaches when they think about facing another encounter with a bully.

People who are bullied might have a hard time sleeping or have nightmares. Their grades may go down. It is hard to focus on schoolwork when you are feeling scared.

Sometimes, bullying can change a victim's **personality**. A friend who has always been easygoing and fun might become angry. They could have an attitude or act **defensively**. Even the smallest issue may cause a big reaction.

A victim of physical bullying might have unexplained injuries, like bruises or scratches. Their possessions might go missing or be destroyed.

Studies Show That...

- 19 percent of students who have been bullied have negative feelings about themselves.
- 14 percent of students who have been bullied say that being bullied has affected their friendships.
- 9 percent of students who have been bullied report a negative impact on their physical health.

Is This Normal?

Bullying happens a lot. Researchers tried to find out how often kids are bullied and who it affects. Here is what they discovered. One out of every five students has been bullied. Boys and girls have an equal chance of getting bullied. Many students who experience cyberbullying also report being bullied at school.

Bullying is common. But it is never normal, and it is never okay. Students, teachers, parents, and others should always take bullying seriously and take actions to protect victims.

When Is Bullying a Problem?

Bullying is always a problem. People who experience bullying on a regular basis have more struggles with **emotional** issues. They might feel ashamed, isolated, and sad. But bullying is never the victim's fault.

Did You Know?
Only 36 percent of students who are bullied report it to an adult.

Sometimes, the problem of bullying becomes **overwhelming**. Repeated bullying can result in depression or severe **anxiety**. A victim may feel hopeless and self-harm or use illegal substances to try to deal with the painful feelings. It is very important for victims to tell someone and get the help they need.

Chapter 4: Strategies for Taking Control

What can you do to stop bullying? Learn some great strategies for taking control.

Strategy #1: Tell an Adult

If you are being bullied, it is important to talk to a trusted adult. It can be scary to ask for help. But your favorite teacher, your parent, your guidance counselor, or your coach can be a great listener.

Remember, this is not tattling about a small problem. Bullying is serious. Getting help is essential for keeping yourself and other kids safe. Explain exactly what is happening and how long it has been going on.

Make sure to report the five Ws:

- ☐ Who: What is the bully's name?
- ☐ What: What happened?
- ☐ When: When did it happen?
- ☐ Where: Where did it happen?
- ☐ Witnesses: Who saw what happened?

If one adult doesn't help, find another adult who will. Keep trying! You deserve support.

There Is Good News!

Many schools have prevention programs and zero tolerance policies to deal with bullying. Schoolwide programs can reduce bullying by 25 percent.

Strategy #2: Be a Friend and Walk with a Friend

Try to walk from one place to another in a group or with a trusted friend. Bullies are more likely to pick on someone if they are alone. The more time you spend with others, the less likely the bully is to approach you. What if you don't have a buddy? Offer to walk with someone else who is alone. You might make a new friend.

Chances are that someone who is bullying you is also being mean to other kids. Watch to see who you can team up with. Talk to the bully's other victims and let them know that you support them. Bullies hate to be outnumbered.

There Is Good News!

Two-thirds of tweens shared that they are willing to help protect someone who is being bullied.

Strategy #3: Avoid the Bully

If you know where a bully hangs out, avoid that area. Take a different path to get to your next class or to reach your destination.

If you do run into a bully, pretend you can't hear them and keep walking away. Try your best to be brave. Keep your head up and walk with confidence. The bully wants attention and wants to make you feel uncomfortable. Don't let this happen! Stay calm and keep control of your emotions.

Strategy #4: Be Brave

Tell the bully, "No!" or "Stop it!" Be confident with your words and body language. Stand tall and hold your head high. Use a comeback like, "Whatever, why are you talking to me?" or "Hey, that's not helpful and it's not okay to talk to me like that." Just state the facts and keep your cool.

You might feel angry or upset. But try to avoid showing your feelings to the bully. Use a strategy like counting backward or spelling words in your head to keep your mind busy and your emotions under control. Try repeating a sentence to yourself like this one: "I may not be perfect, but at least I'm not a bully!"

Don't know what to say to a bully? Try these ideas.

- ☑ Really?
- ☑ Excuse me?
- ☑ Um, whatever.
- ☑ Okay, so...
- ☑ I heard you. I just don't care.
- ☑ Are you finished now?
- ☑ You can talk, but I'm not listening.
- ☑ Say what you want. Doesn't make it true.
- ☑ I just feel sorry for you.
- ☑ You figured out I'm different than you. You are so smart!

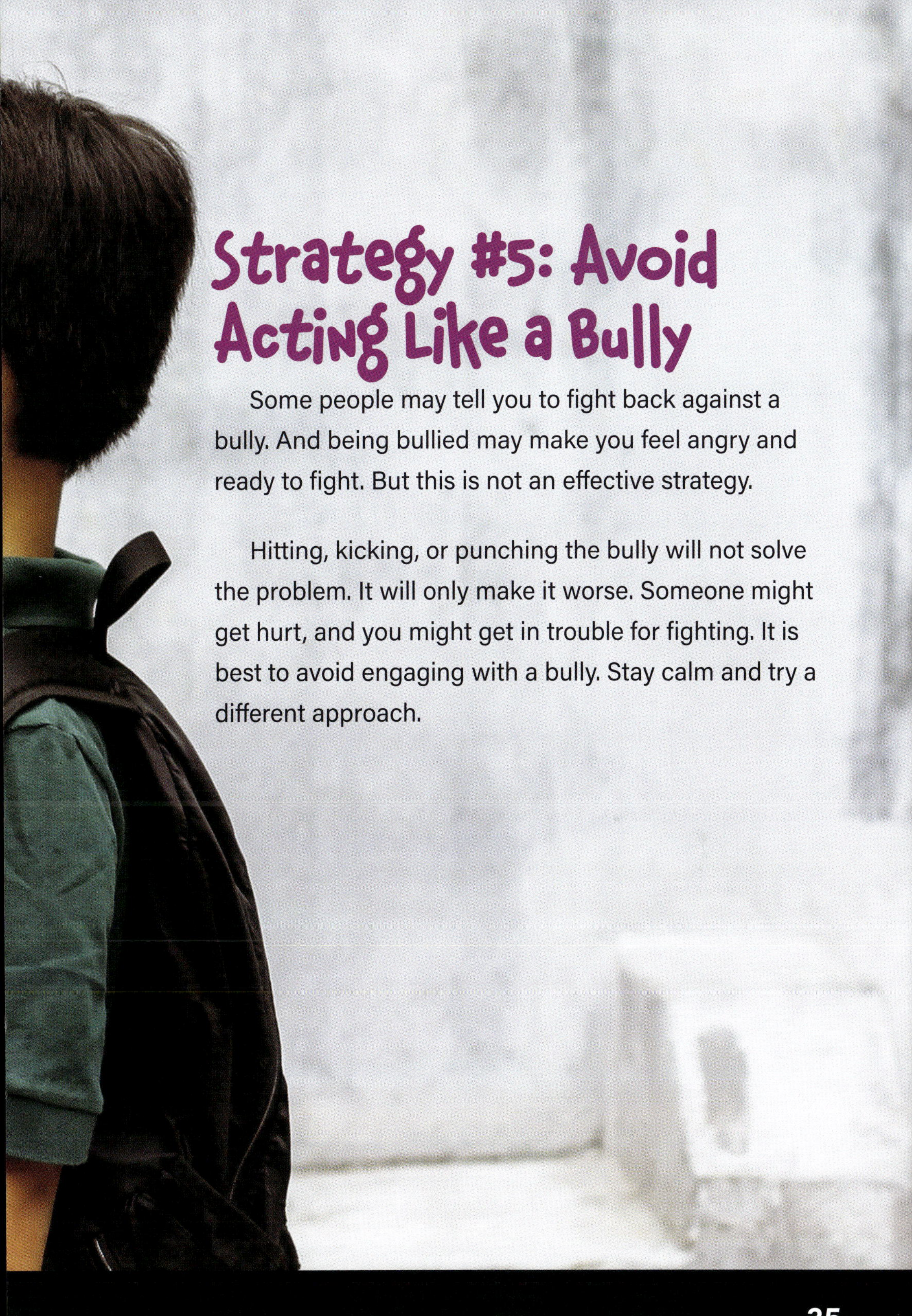

Strategy #5: Avoid Acting Like a Bully

Some people may tell you to fight back against a bully. And being bullied may make you feel angry and ready to fight. But this is not an effective strategy.

Hitting, kicking, or punching the bully will not solve the problem. It will only make it worse. Someone might get hurt, and you might get in trouble for fighting. It is best to avoid engaging with a bully. Stay calm and try a different approach.

Strategy #6: Be an upstander

People who are witnesses to bullying are called bystanders. A bystander just watches the event without getting involved. They don't stand up for the victim. Bystanders are part of the problem. This is especially true when a bystander's first reaction to bullying is to capture it on a video.

An upstander is someone who jumps to action when they see someone getting bullied. They show support and kindness for the victim. Kids who are supported by their **peers** are less likely to experience anxiety or stress.

What Do Upstanders Do?

- ☑ They use humor to redirect the conversation.
- ☑ They question the bully's behavior to shift the focus off the victim.
- ☑ They keep the victim company and provide support.
- ☑ They check on the victim after the incident.
- ☑ They show that they care.

Chapter 5: Dealing with Bullying

Remember Kayla? She decided to talk to her guidance counselor and ask for help. She shared what happened, and they came up with a plan together. Kayla decided not to give power to her bullies. She can eat lunch with a different group of friends at another table in the cafeteria. If she sees her bullies, she will not show them she is angry or upset because that is probably what they want to see. She will tell them in a clear voice that she isn't going to be bothered by their attacks and walk away. Having a plan makes Kayla feel powerful. She knows she can gain control over the situation.

Remember Jason? He also came up with a plan to stop his bully. He talked to his math teacher, Mr. Lopez. Jason trusted him, and he knew the teacher would listen to him and believe him. It turned out that Mr. Lopez had heard other kids talk about being bullied by the same student. He promised to watch out for the bully and to let the principal know to keep an eye out as well.

Mr. Lopez recommended that Jason always walk with another student or teacher in the hallways. The bully will be less likely to approach him when he is around other people. If he does run into the bully, Jason decided to say loudly and confidently, "No, you can't talk to me that way," and walk away. Mr. Lopez helped Jason practice so that he would be ready.

Remember: It is never okay to be harmed physically, socially, or verbally by anyone else. You can learn to deal with a bully!

YOUR TURN: HOW DO YOU DEAL WITH BULLYING?

For each situation, select the answer that best describes you. Make a note of your answers on a separate sheet of paper.

1. There is a kid at school who keeps pushing people in the hallways.

A. This kid has pushed you every day this week. You get a stomachache when you think about going to school and seeing him again.

B. This kid pushed you yesterday. You try to avoid him whenever you can.

C. You have heard about this kid. You and your friends choose to walk a different way to avoid him.

D. You have heard about this kid. You and your friends talk to an adult. Teachers now stand in the hallway to watch as kids walk by.

2. There's a new student at school. She looks different and has a hard time making friends. Online, people are posting photos of her with rude comments.

A. You were once new at school. The popular kids made fun of your clothes and hair. You ignore what is happening to the new student.

B. You hear people making fun of the new student. You want to be sure they don't say anything bad about you, so you laugh along with them.

C. You see that the new student is scared and lonely. You and your friends talk to her and invite her to have lunch with you.

D. You overhear people laughing about the new student. You tell them to give her a chance. You ask the new student to join you for lunch.

3. Your friends are sending mean texts about you. This hurts your feelings. What do you do?

A. Nothing. You must have done something wrong to make your friends feel that way about you.

B. Send mean texts about them. You want to get even.

C. Talk to your mom. Work together to come up with a plan to stop the texts.

D. Tell your friends that what they are doing needs to stop. Talk to your guidance counselor and ask for help to feel safe at school and make the texts stop.

4. An older boy waits for the younger kids to get off the bus and start walking home. He takes their things and threatens to hurt them.

A. You don't want to be the target of his bullying, so you join in the threatening behaviors.

B. You watch what he does to the younger students. You are afraid.

C. You walk home with the younger students. You share with them that staying in a group is safer.

D. You talk to the bus driver. She now only lets students off in groups, and she watches them walk away. You walk along with the younger students.

Think about your answers.

If you chose mostly A: It is likely that you are being bullied or have been bullied in the past. You are not alone! Talk to a trusted adult to get help and support.

If you chose mostly B: You may be the target of bullying behavior. You can deal with bullies! Use the strategies in this book to help.

If you chose mostly C: You are familiar with bullying or have seen bullying behavior. You are on the right track. Take steps to keep yourself and your friends safe.

If you chose mostly D: You are fortunate to have little or no interaction with bullies. Support those around you who might have to deal with bullies.

Exploration and Discovery: Activities to Try

1. Think about three people who are different than you or who you don't know very well. Write down one nice thing about each person.
2. Write three actions you can take to help prevent bullying online or in school. Choose at least one and carry it out.
3. Create a short anti-bullying video. In it, explain what bullying looks like and give one tip that someone can follow to stay safe. Talk to your parents about posting the video online or sharing it with others.
4. Sometimes, people are bullied because they are different. But being different is something to celebrate! Think of two things that are unique about you. Write about how those two things can positively influence other people.
5. Create a cartoon or a poster that shows how to deal with a bully. Share your artwork with someone you know.

YOU ARE NOT ALONE

Being bullied can make you feel hopeless and alone. But you are NOT alone. There are good people who care about you and want to help. There are also many resources you can use to learn more and help yourself.

Explore some of these ways to find the kindness and support you deserve.

People to Ask for Help

☑ guidance counselor
☑ teacher
☑ principal
☑ assistant principal
☑ parent
☑ older sibling
☑ grandparent
☑ aunt or uncle
☑ coach
☑ school secretary
☑ bus driver
☑ religious youth group leader
☑ any friend that you trust
☑ any adult that you trust

Websites

Pacer Center's Kids Against Bullying

www.pacerkidsagainstbullying.org

Meet a crew of characters who are like people you know and who have found ways to deal with bullies. Read messages of support posted by young people who care.

Stomp Out Bullying

www.stompoutbullying.org

At this in-depth website, watch videos, find a HelpChat Crisis Line, learn about the World Day of Bullying Prevention, and more.

Stop Bullying

www.stopbullying.gov/kids

At this government website, you can watch videos that show how to stop bullies and celebrate differences.

Books

Kaufman, Gershen, and Lev Raphael. *Stick Up for Yourself!: Every Kid's Guide to Personal Power and Positive Self-Esteem*. Minneapolis, MN: Free Spirit Publishing, 2019.

Speer, Jessica. *The Phone Book: Stay Safe, Be Smart, and Make the World Better with the Powerful Device in Your Hand*. Sanger, CA: Familius Publishing, 2023.

Woody, Jessica. *Anti-Bullying Book for Girls: Practical Tools to Manage Bullying and Build Confidence*. New York, NY: Rockridge Press, 2021.

Phone Helplines

Crisis Text Line

Text HOME to 741741 or message on WhatsApp. Young people of color can text STEVE to 741741 to reach culturally trained counselors.

LGBT National Youth Talkline

1-800-246-7743

National Suicide Prevention Lifeline

1-800-273-8255

Suicide and Crisis Lifeline

Call or text 988.

GLOSSARY

aggressive (uh-GRES-iv)
Showing fierce or threatening behavior

aggressors (uh-GRES-urs)
People who are pushy and ready to attack

anxiety (ang-ZYE-i-tee)
Feelings of worry or fear

cortisol (KOR-tuh-suhl)
A hormone produced by the adrenal glands when the body is under stress

defensively (di-FEN-siv-lee)
In a manner that rejects challenge or criticism; protectively

emotional (i-MOH-shuh-nuhl)
Of or having to do with feelings

hippocampus (hip-oh-CAMP-us)
A region of the brain that is the center of emotions and memory

hormone (HOR-mone)
A chemical made by the body that affects growth, development, and behavior

instigated (IN-sti-gay-tid)
Started something, especially something that leads to trouble

intimidate (in-TIM-i-date)
To frighten someone, especially in order to make them do something

overwhelming (oh-vur-WELM-ing)
Having a strong effect or impact

peers (peerz)
People of your same age or status

personality (pur-suh-NAL-i-tee)
All of the qualities or traits that make one person different from others

self-conscious (self KAHN-shuhs)
Worried or concerned about what people think of you

stress (stres)
Worry, strain, or pressure

target (TAHR-git)
Someone who is criticized or made fun of

victim (VIK-tuhm)
A person who is hurt, harmed, or made to suffer

violent (VYE-uh-luhnt)
Showing physical force meant to cause harm

INDEX

ABOUT THE AUTHOR

Kelli Hicks is a teacher, mom, and author who lives in Tampa, Florida. She was bullied in middle school and knows how painful that feeling can be. She works hard to make sure her students and her kids feel safe and know that she will help them if they are confronted by a bully. Her dog, Emma June, tries to bully her into giving her treats as often as she can.